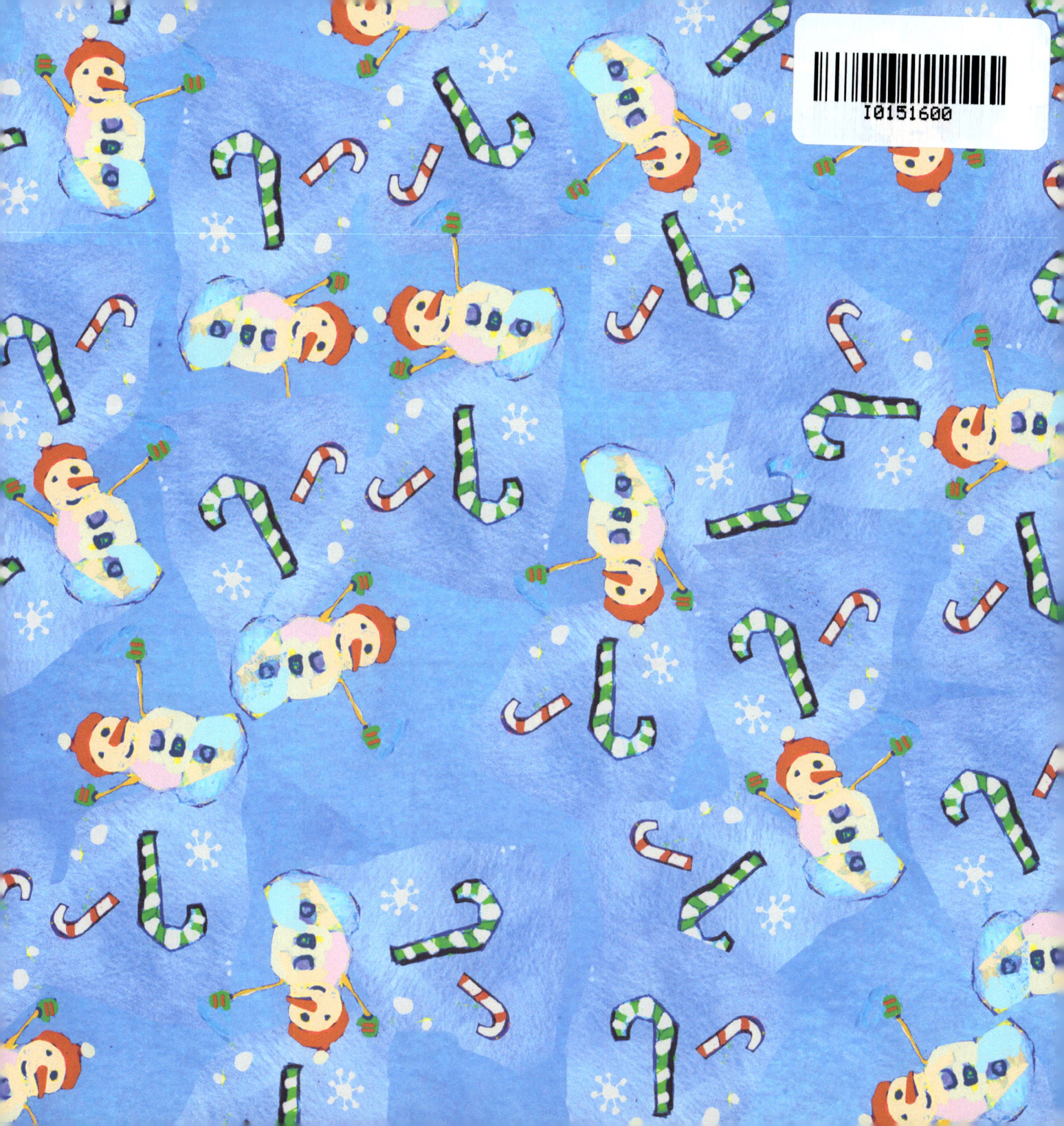

In this Moment

Celebrating The Holidays

By C. Valentine

Illustrations R. Freeland

This Book Belongs To:

_____

Table of Contents

Year:_____

THIS HOLIDAY SEASON

♪ Sounds like:_____ 🎄 Smells like:_____ 👁 Looks like:_____

🍬 Tastes like:_____ 🔵 Feels like:_____

HOLIDAY FAVORITES

Food:_____

Song:_____

Game:_____

Decoration:_____

Gift given:_____

Gift received:_____

Activity:_____

Tradition:_____

THE SEASON'S TOP THREE SPECIAL MOMENTS

1._____

2._____

3._____

If I could give a gift to the world this Holiday Season it would be:_____

_____

If I could have one wish come true this Holiday Season it would be:_____

_____

2

HERE'S HOW I'LL REMEMBER THIS HOLIDAY SEASON...

Year:_____

THIS HOLIDAY SEASON

♪ Sounds like:_____   🎄 Smells like:_____   👁 Looks like:_____

🍬 Tastes like:_____   🔵 Feels like:_____

HOLIDAY FAVORITES

Food:_____

Song:_____

Game:_____

Decoration:_____

Gift given:_____

Gift received:_____

Activity:_____

Tradition:_____

THE SEASON'S TOP THREE SPECIAL MOMENTS

1._____

2._____

3._____

If I could give a gift to the world this Holiday Season it would be:_____

_____

If I could have one wish come true this Holiday Season it would be:_____

_____

4

HERE'S HOW I'LL REMEMBER THIS HOLIDAY SEASON...

Year:_____

THIS HOLIDAY SEASON

♪ Sounds like:_____ 🎄 Smells like:_____ 👁 Looks like:_____

🍬 Tastes like:_____ 🔵 Feels like:_____

HOLIDAY FAVORITES

Food:_____

Song:_____

Game:_____

Decoration:_____

Gift given:_____

Gift received:_____

Activity:_____

Tradition:_____

THE SEASON'S TOP THREE SPECIAL MOMENTS

1._____

2._____

3._____

If I could give a gift to the world this Holiday Season it would be:_____
_____

If I could have one wish come true this Holiday Season it would be:_____
_____

6

HERE'S HOW I'LL REMEMBER THIS HOLIDAY SEASON...

Year:_____

THIS HOLIDAY SEASON

♪ Sounds like:_____   🎄 Smells like:_____   👁 Looks like:_____

🍬 Tastes like:_____   🔵 Feels like:_____

HOLIDAY FAVORITES

Food:_____

Song:_____

Game:_____

Decoration:_____

Gift given:_____

Gift received:_____

Activity:_____

Tradition:_____

THE SEASON'S TOP THREE SPECIAL MOMENTS

1._____

2._____

3._____

If I could give a gift to the world this Holiday Season it would be:_____
_____

If I could have one wish come true this Holiday Season it would be:_____
_____

8

HERE'S HOW I'LL REMEMBER THIS HOLIDAY SEASON...

Year:_____

THIS HOLIDAY SEASON

Sounds like:_____ Smells like:_____ Looks like:_____

Tastes like:_____ Feels like:_____

HOLIDAY FAVORITES

Food:_____

Song:_____

Game:_____

Decoration:_____

Gift given:_____

Gift received:_____

Activity:_____

Tradition:_____

THE SEASON'S TOP THREE SPECIAL MOMENTS

1._____

2._____

3._____

If I could give a gift to the world this Holiday Season it would be:_____

_____

If I could have one wish come true this Holiday Season it would be: _____

_____

HERE'S HOW I'LL REMEMBER THIS HOLIDAY SEASON...

Year:_____

THIS HOLIDAY SEASON

♪ Sounds like:_____ 🎄 Smells like:_____ 👁 Looks like:_____

🍬 Tastes like:_____ 🔵 Feels like:_____

HOLIDAY FAVORITES

Food:_____

Song:_____

Game:_____

Decoration:_____

Gift given:_____

Gift received:_____

Activity:_____

Tradition:_____

THE SEASON'S TOP THREE SPECIAL MOMENTS

1._____

2._____

3._____

If I could give a gift to the world this Holiday Season it would be:_____

_____

If I could have one wish come true this Holiday Season it would be:_____

_____

HERE'S HOW I'LL REMEMBER THIS HOLIDAY SEASON...

13

Year:_____

THIS HOLIDAY SEASON

♪ Sounds like:_____ 🎄 Smells like:_____ 👁 Looks like:_____

🍬 Tastes like:_____ 🔮 Feels like:_____

HOLIDAY FAVORITES

Food:_____

Song:_____

Game:_____

Decoration:_____

Gift given:_____

Gift received:_____

Activity:_____

Tradition:_____

THE SEASON'S TOP THREE SPECIAL MOMENTS

1._____

2._____

3._____

If I could give a gift to the world this Holiday Season it would be:_____

_____

If I could have one wish come true this Holiday Season it would be: _____

_____

14

HERE'S HOW I'LL REMEMBER THIS HOLIDAY SEASON...

Year:_____

THIS HOLIDAY SEASON

♪ Sounds like:_____ 🎄 Smells like:_____ 👁 Looks like:_____

🍬 Tastes like:_____ 🔵 Feels like:_____

HOLIDAY FAVORITES

Food:_____

Song:_____

Game:_____

Decoration:_____

Gift given:_____

Gift received:_____

Activity:_____

Tradition:_____

THE SEASON'S TOP THREE SPECIAL MOMENTS

🔵 1._____

🟢 2._____

⚫ 3._____

If I could give a gift to the world this Holiday Season it would be:_____

_____

If I could have one wish come true this Holiday Season it would be:_____

_____

HERE'S HOW I'LL REMEMBER THIS HOLIDAY SEASON...

Year:_____

THIS HOLIDAY SEASON

♪ Sounds like:_____ 🎄 Smells like:_____ 👁 Looks like:_____

🍬 Tastes like:_____ 🔵 Feels like:_____

HOLIDAY FAVORITES

Food:_____

Song:_____

Game:_____

Decoration:_____

Gift given:_____

Gift received:_____

Activity:_____

Tradition:_____

THE SEASON'S TOP THREE SPECIAL MOMENTS

🔵 1._____

🟢 2._____

🔵 3._____

If I could give a gift to the world this Holiday Season it would be:_____

_____

If I could have one wish come true this Holiday Season it would be:____

_____

18

HERE'S HOW I'LL REMEMBER THIS HOLIDAY SEASON...

Year:_____

THIS HOLIDAY SEASON

♪ Sounds like:_____ 🎄 Smells like:_____ 👁 Looks like:_____

🍬 Tastes like:_____ 🔵 Feels like:_____

HOLIDAY FAVORITES

Food:_____

Song:_____

Game:_____

Decoration:_____

Gift given:_____

Gift received:_____

Activity:_____

Tradition:_____

THE SEASON'S TOP THREE SPECIAL MOMENTS

1._____

2._____

3._____

If I could give a gift to the world this Holiday Season it would be:_____

_____

If I could have one wish come true this Holiday Season it would be:_____

_____

HERE'S HOW I'LL REMEMBER THIS HOLIDAY SEASON...

Year:_____

THIS HOLIDAY SEASON

♪ Sounds like:_____ 🎄 Smells like:_____ 👁 Looks like:_____

🍬 Tastes like:_____ 🔵 Feels like:_____

HOLIDAY FAVORITES

Food:_____

Song:_____

Game:_____

Decoration:_____

Gift given:_____

Gift received:_____

Activity:_____

Tradition:_____

THE SEASON'S TOP THREE SPECIAL MOMENTS

1._____

2._____

3._____

If I could give a gift to the world this Holiday Season it would be:_____
_____

If I could have one wish come true this Holiday Season it would be: ____
_____

HERE'S HOW I'LL REMEMBER THIS HOLIDAY SEASON...

Year:_____

THIS HOLIDAY SEASON

♪ Sounds like:_____ 🎄 Smells like:_____ 👁 Looks like:_____

🍬 Tastes like:_____ 🎄 Feels like:_____

HOLIDAY FAVORITES

Food:_____

Song:_____

Game:_____

Decoration:_____

Gift given:_____

Gift received:_____

Activity:_____

Tradition:_____

THE SEASON'S TOP THREE SPECIAL MOMENTS

1._____

2._____

3._____

If I could give a gift to the world this Holiday Season it would be:_____

_____

If I could have one wish come true this Holiday Season it would be:_____

_____

HERE'S HOW I'LL REMEMBER THIS HOLIDAY SEASON...

Year:_____

THIS HOLIDAY SEASON

♪ Sounds like:_____ 🎄 Smells like:_____ 👁 Looks like:_____

🍭 Tastes like:_____ 🔵 Feels like:_____

HOLIDAY FAVORITES

Food:_____

Song:_____

Game:_____

Decoration:_____

Gift given:_____

Gift received:_____

Activity:_____

Tradition:_____

THE SEASON'S TOP THREE SPECIAL MOMENTS

1._____

2._____

3._____

If I could give a gift to the world this Holiday Season it would be:_____
_____

If I could have one wish come true this Holiday Season it would be:_____
_____

HERE'S HOW I'LL REMEMBER THIS HOLIDAY SEASON...

Year:_____

THIS HOLIDAY SEASON

♪ Sounds like:_____ 🎄 Smells like:_____ 👁 Looks like:_____

🍬 Tastes like:_____ 🔵 Feels like:_____

HOLIDAY FAVORITES

Food:_____

Song:_____

Game:_____

Decoration:_____

Gift given:_____

Gift received:_____

Activity:_____

Tradition:_____

THE SEASON'S TOP THREE SPECIAL MOMENTS

1._____

2._____

3._____

If I could give a gift to the world this Holiday Season it would be:_____

_____

If I could have one wish come true this Holiday Season it would be:_____

_____

28

HERE'S HOW I'LL REMEMBER THIS HOLIDAY SEASON...

Year:_____

THIS HOLIDAY SEASON

♪ Sounds like:_____ 🎄 Smells like:_____ 👁 Looks like:_____

🍬 Tastes like:_____ 🔵 Feels like:_____

HOLIDAY FAVORITES

Food:_____

Song:_____

Game:_____

Decoration:_____

Gift given:_____

Gift received:_____

Activity:_____

Tradition:_____

THE SEASON'S TOP THREE SPECIAL MOMENTS

1._____

2._____

3._____

If I could give a gift to the world this Holiday Season it would be:_____
_____

If I could have one wish come true this Holiday Season it would be: ____
_____

HERE'S HOW I'LL REMEMBER THIS HOLIDAY SEASON...

Year:_____

THIS HOLIDAY SEASON

♫ Sounds like:_____   🎄 Smells like:_____   👁 Looks like:_____

🍬 Tastes like:_____   🔵 Feels like:_____

HOLIDAY FAVORITES

Food:_____

Song:_____

Game:_____

Decoration:_____

Gift given:_____

Gift received:_____

Activity:_____

Tradition:_____

THE SEASON'S TOP THREE SPECIAL MOMENTS

1._____

2._____

3._____

If I could give a gift to the world this Holiday Season it would be:_____

_____

If I could have one wish come true this Holiday Season it would be:_____

_____

HERE'S HOW I'LL REMEMBER THIS HOLIDAY SEASON...

Year:_____

THIS HOLIDAY SEASON

♫ Sounds like:_____ 🎄 Smells like:_____ 👁 Looks like:_____

🍬 Tastes like:_____ 🎄 Feels like:_____

HOLIDAY FAVORITES

Food:_____

Song:_____

Game:_____

Decoration:_____

Gift given:_____

Gift received:_____

Activity:_____

Tradition:_____

THE SEASON'S TOP THREE SPECIAL MOMENTS

1._____

2._____

3._____

If I could give a gift to the world this Holiday Season it would be:_____

_____

If I could have one wish come true this Holiday Season it would be: ____

_____

34

HERE'S HOW I'LL REMEMBER THIS HOLIDAY SEASON...

Year:_____

THIS HOLIDAY SEASON

♪ Sounds like:_____ 🎄 Smells like:_____ 👁 Looks like:_____

🍬 Tastes like:_____ 🔵 Feels like:_____

HOLIDAY FAVORITES

Food:_____

Song:_____

Game:_____

Decoration:_____

Gift given:_____

Gift received:_____

Activity:_____

Tradition:_____

THE SEASON'S TOP THREE SPECIAL MOMENTS

1._____

2._____

3._____

If I could give a gift to the world this Holiday Season it would be:_____
_____

If I could have one wish come true this Holiday Season it would be:____
_____

HERE'S HOW I'LL REMEMBER THIS HOLIDAY SEASON...

Year:_____

THIS HOLIDAY SEASON

♪ Sounds like:_____ 🎄 Smells like:_____ 👁 Looks like:_____

🍬 Tastes like:_____ 🔵 Feels like:_____

HOLIDAY FAVORITES

Food:_____

Song:_____

Game:_____

Decoration:_____

Gift given:_____

Gift received:_____

Activity:_____

Tradition:_____

THE SEASON'S TOP THREE SPECIAL MOMENTS

1._____

2._____

3._____

If I could give a gift to the world this Holiday Season it would be:_____

_____

If I could have one wish come true this Holiday Season it would be: _____

_____

HERE'S HOW I'LL REMEMBER THIS HOLIDAY SEASON...

Year:_____

THIS HOLIDAY SEASON

♪ Sounds like:_____ 🎄 Smells like:_____ 👁 Looks like:_____

🍬 Tastes like:_____ 🔵 Feels like:_____

HOLIDAY FAVORITES

Food:_____

Song:_____

Game:_____

Decoration:_____

Gift given:_____

Gift received:_____

Activity:_____

Tradition:_____

THE SEASON'S TOP THREE SPECIAL MOMENTS

1._____

2._____

3._____

If I could give a gift to the world this Holiday Season it would be:_____

_____

If I could have one wish come true this Holiday Season it would be:____

_____

40

HERE'S HOW I'LL REMEMBER THIS HOLIDAY SEASON...

Year:_____

THIS HOLIDAY SEASON

♫ Sounds like:_____ 🎄 Smells like:_____ 👁 Looks like:_____

🍬 Tastes like:_____ 🔵 Feels like:_____

HOLIDAY FAVORITES

Food:_____

Song:_____

Game:_____

Decoration:_____

Gift given:_____

Gift received:_____

Activity:_____

Tradition:_____

THE SEASON'S TOP THREE SPECIAL MOMENTS

🔵 1._____

🟢 2._____

🔵 3._____

If I could give a gift to the world this Holiday Season it would be:_____

_____

If I could have one wish come true this Holiday Season it would be: ____

_____

HERE'S HOW I'LL REMEMBER THIS HOLIDAY SEASON...

Year:_____

THIS HOLIDAY SEASON

♪ Sounds like:_____ 🎄 Smells like:_____ 👁 Looks like:_____

🍬 Tastes like:_____ 🔵 Feels like:_____

HOLIDAY FAVORITES

Food:_____

Song:_____

Game:_____

Decoration:_____

Gift given:_____

Gift received:_____

Activity:_____

Tradition:_____

THE SEASON'S TOP THREE SPECIAL MOMENTS

🔵 1._____

🟢 2._____

🔵 3._____

If I could give a gift to the world this Holiday Season it would be:_____
_____

If I could have one wish come true this Holiday Season it would be:_____
_____

44

HERE'S HOW I'LL REMEMBER THIS HOLIDAY SEASON...

45

Year:_____

THIS HOLIDAY SEASON

♪ Sounds like:_____ 🎄 Smells like:_____ 👁 Looks like:_____

🍬 Tastes like:_____ 🔵 Feels like:_____

HOLIDAY FAVORITES

Food:_____

Song:_____

Game:_____

Decoration:_____

Gift given:_____

Gift received:_____

Activity:_____

Tradition:_____

THE SEASON'S TOP THREE SPECIAL MOMENTS

1._____

2._____

3._____

If I could give a gift to the world this Holiday Season it would be:_____
_____

If I could have one wish come true this Holiday Season it would be: ____
_____

HERE'S HOW I'LL REMEMBER THIS HOLIDAY SEASON...

Year:_____

THIS HOLIDAY SEASON

♫ Sounds like:_____ 🎄 Smells like:_____ 👁 Looks like:_____

🍬 Tastes like:_____ 🔵 Feels like:_____

HOLIDAY FAVORITES

Food:_____

Song:_____

Game:_____

Decoration:_____

Gift given:_____

Gift received:_____

Activity:_____

Tradition:_____

THE SEASON'S TOP THREE SPECIAL MOMENTS

1._____

2._____

3._____

If I could give a gift to the world this Holiday Season it would be:_____

_____

If I could have one wish come true this Holiday Season it would be: _____

_____

48

HERE'S HOW I'LL REMEMBER THIS HOLIDAY SEASON...

Year:_____

THIS HOLIDAY SEASON

♪ Sounds like:_____ 🎄 Smells like:_____ 👁 Looks like:_____

🍬 Tastes like:_____ 🔵 Feels like:_____

HOLIDAY FAVORITES

Food:_____

Song:_____

Game:_____

Decoration:_____

Gift given:_____

Gift received:_____

Activity:_____

Tradition:_____

THE SEASON'S TOP THREE SPECIAL MOMENTS

1._____

2._____

3._____

If I could give a gift to the world this Holiday Season it would be:_____

_____

If I could have one wish come true this Holiday Season it would be:____

_____

HERE'S HOW I'LL REMEMBER THIS HOLIDAY SEASON...

Year:_____

THIS HOLIDAY SEASON

♪ Sounds like:_____ 🎄 Smells like:_____ 👁 Looks like:_____

🍬 Tastes like:_____ 🎄 Feels like:_____

HOLIDAY FAVORITES

Food:_____

Song:_____

Game:_____

Decoration:_____

Gift given:_____

Gift received:_____

Activity:_____

Tradition:_____

THE SEASON'S TOP THREE SPECIAL MOMENTS

1._____

2._____

3._____

If I could give a gift to the world this Holiday Season it would be:_____
_____

If I could have one wish come true this Holiday Season it would be:____
_____

52

HERE'S HOW I'LL REMEMBER THIS HOLIDAY SEASON...

Year:_____

THIS HOLIDAY SEASON

♫ Sounds like:_____ 🎄 Smells like:_____ 👁 Looks like:_____

🍬 Tastes like:_____ 🔵 Feels like:_____

HOLIDAY FAVORITES

Food:_____

Song:_____

Game:_____

Decoration:_____

Gift given:_____

Gift received:_____

Activity:_____

Tradition:_____

THE SEASON'S TOP THREE SPECIAL MOMENTS

1._____

2._____

3._____

If I could give a gift to the world this Holiday Season it would be:_____

_____

If I could have one wish come true this Holiday Season it would be:_____

_____

HERE'S HOW I'LL REMEMBER THIS HOLIDAY SEASON...

Year:_____

THIS HOLIDAY SEASON

♪ Sounds like:_____ 🎄 Smells like:_____ 👁 Looks like:_____

🍬 Tastes like:_____ 🔵 Feels like:_____

HOLIDAY FAVORITES

Food:_____

Song:_____

Game:_____

Decoration:_____

Gift given:_____

Gift received:_____

Activity:_____

Tradition:_____

THE SEASON'S TOP THREE SPECIAL MOMENTS

🔵 1._____

🟢 2._____

🔵 3._____

If I could give a gift to the world this Holiday Season it would be:_____

_____

If I could have one wish come true this Holiday Season it would be:_____

_____

HERE'S HOW I'LL REMEMBER THIS HOLIDAY SEASON...

Year:_____

THIS HOLIDAY SEASON

♪ Sounds like:_____ 🎄 Smells like:_____ 👁 Looks like:_____

🍬 Tastes like:_____ 🔵 Feels like:_____

HOLIDAY FAVORITES

Food:_____

Song:_____

Game:_____

Decoration:_____

Gift given:_____

Gift received:_____

Activity:_____

Tradition:_____

THE SEASON'S TOP THREE SPECIAL MOMENTS

1._____

2._____

3._____

If I could give a gift to the world this Holiday Season it would be:_____

_____

If I could have one wish come true this Holiday Season it would be:_____

_____

HERE'S HOW I'LL REMEMBER THIS HOLIDAY SEASON...

Year:_____

THIS HOLIDAY SEASON

♪ Sounds like:_____ 🎄 Smells like:_____ 👁 Looks like:_____

🍬 Tastes like:_____ 🔵 Feels like:_____

HOLIDAY FAVORITES

Food:_____

Song:_____

Game:_____

Decoration:_____

Gift given:_____

Gift received:_____

Activity:_____

Tradition:_____

THE SEASON'S TOP THREE SPECIAL MOMENTS

1._____

2._____

3._____

If I could give a gift to the world this Holiday Season it would be:_____
_____

If I could have one wish come true this Holiday Season it would be:____
_____

HERE'S HOW I'LL REMEMBER THIS HOLIDAY SEASON...

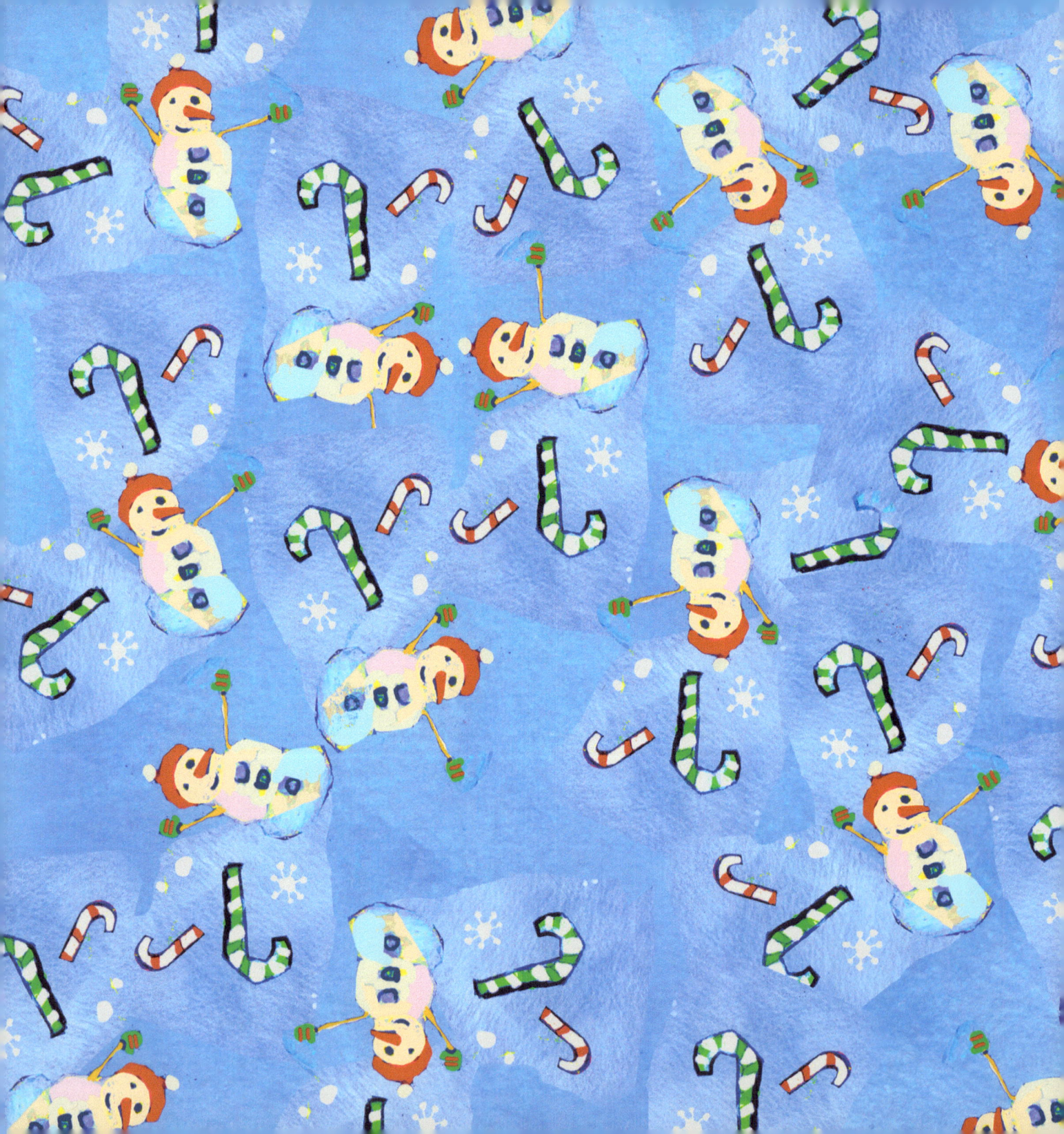